Flying Since Covid

This Essential Guide
Will Save Your Journey

W0073298

Claire Petit

As a full-time traveler, Claire shares her knowledge and experiences on the German travel blog bluebayou.co.

Table of Content

Welcome to the New Normal

New normal? This is a term that I don't like at all, but it is widely used in Asia. So, if you, in the summer of 2020, were still hoping that this whole thing was going to end one day, you can bury this thought—at least when it comes to traveling to this part of the world.

I've flown about 200 times in my life. Before Covid, everything always went smoothly, both actively and passively witnessed at airports. I had the wrong flight time in mind a total of three times and almost missed my plane. Also, my companions appeared so late twice that I heard my name as a "last call." Since Covid, however, despite intensive preparation, I have twice experienced the situation that I almost did not get through the check-in, and about ten times observed people who did *not* come on board the flights they paid for. I also know several people who were denied entry after landing and then had to fly back. And more importantly, I saved the flights of several people by talking to them about all the requirements and making sure they took the right Covid test in time.

Traveling once was fun for me. As a full-time traveler, it would basically be fatal to claim otherwise. However, I am currently on the way, yet far away from saying so. Traveling is no longer fun. Neither for me nor for many others, especially since summer 2021. With the vaccinations, so many requirements came up, and each country has its own ideas about what entry measures can protect its citizens from Covid.

We have made an insane leap yet, at the same time, a step backward in terms of technology. While countries like China monitor every step with their tracking apps to calculate the danger posed by the individual regarding Covid, Thailand temporarily did not let you into the country unless you were able to present a full-page printed QR code, as scanning that from a mobile phone would have been too easy. While Malaysia can no longer be entered without a current smartphone with a special Covid tracking app installed before departure and registered on oneself, Cambodia also demanded printouts on paper for a while—without even keeping those. At airports, there are sometimes Covid-related "copy shops," which offer printouts to devastated travelers' for around 40 USD per page...

One thing Covid has taught us while traveling: it has never made more sense to talk to those who have just landed in the country we aim to go to. Experience has never been more valuable. That's why this book is needed. I write it in such a fundamental way that it will not be outdated after two weeks but has the potential to save you your journey in the long term. I'll teach you what you must think about when traveling during a pandemic.

1   Before Booking a Flight

In the past, you could just book a flight and travel; of course, more or less complicated depending on the country. This has become way more difficult as there is so much to consider and read. Good preparation ensures a mainly carefree journey, whereby I would still be quite careful with the word "fun." So, there are a few things to consider before you book a flight...

1.1   Good Old Money

I primarily use skyscanner.de to find the lowest prices for my flights. The German version very often provides much cheaper results than the .com version. This website does not cover insane sales, which, for example, low-cost airlines organize very often, but you get a good overview of what's possible. Red marked "self-transfer" flights are displayed at really low prices. It means booking two separate flights to get a lower overall price. Therefore, the baggage must be checked in again during the stopover by yourself—it will not be forwarded to the final destination, even if it is the same airline. This approach was simple and cheap before Covid.

Now, however, it has become very important whether you are traveling with checked baggage. If this is the case, depending on quarantine or entry requirements, you may *no longer* be able to simply leave the security area to pick up and re-check your luggage. If, for example, a country requires the booking of a quarantine hotel or a test on arrival, you will only be able to get through immigration with this proof; otherwise, you will not be able to check in your baggage for your connecting flight. Therefore, special care should be taken here, especially since the rules can change daily. I would rather not book such a self-transfer flight anymore. So, make sure to book a flight in which your luggage is forwarded straight to your final destination, or be aware of the risk of possible additional costs if you have to leave the security area.

It also makes sense to check how much a Covid test costs in the destination country, should one be necessary for your way back. Cambodia, for example, is one of the poorest countries in the world, which is why I would have never expected the PCR tests there to cost almost three times as much as in Germany. Checking can be useful if you do not want to exceed a certain budget and want to exclude unpleasant surprises as much as possible. Please be aware that the rules are volatile, and the prices can fluctuate significantly, even within one city. In Germany, for example, there are often prices between 50 and 150 USD for the same test within one city.

1.2   Verification of Entry Requirements

I have now met several people who found extremely cheap flights or holiday offers online, did not check the entry requirements, and could not go on that vacation in the end. Two even arrived in the destination country, as the airlines probably didn't care, and were then sent back home right away. I saw incredibly cheap deals for Seychelles in 2021. So cheap that I almost booked directly. But then I wondered where the catch was, did quick research, and learned that they would not allow any tourists to the country. So, yes, I could have booked the flights, but I would never have been able to enter the country. It is, therefore, highly important to check the entry requirements before each booking and to be aware that they can change at any time.

If you use Google, it is almost always enough to type in the keyword "Entry [country name]" to get to an official government page showing recent entry requirements as the first search result. However, I know of one case in which the information provided by the Federal Foreign Office had *not* been correctly updated and did not show the newly added ban for tourists.

Simple research is not enough for me. I also like to cross-check with the information I find from at least one major airline flying to the country in question and the information that, for example, the UK provides for its travelers.

If that's still not enough for you, I recommend searching Instagram for "[pin emoji] [country name or city name for metropolises like Bangkok]." So, your destination with a pin emoji in front of it. Before my trip to Thailand, I did this and contacted several people who had just flown to Bangkok to find out what is strictly controlled at arrival and how. This was the only way I learned that a usual PCR test would not work to get in. Information that saved my entry. More on that later. This approach has a nice side effect: you can gain great new contacts.

1.3   Country Reopening's

To find out whether a previously closed country is reopening, I primarily use the Google News search with the search term "[country name] reopening." Here you will find the latest information in English that has been published concerning the country. You can do the same with "[country name] quarantine" to find out if quarantine regulations have changed. Be sure to pay attention to the information that applies to your vaccination status. Also, check if a reopening applies for tourists or business travelers only.

1.4   Transit Only with Certain Airlines

Singapore has shown the way with its Vaccinated Travel Lanes (VTL): it can happen that a country only allows transit with certain approved airlines. This does *not* mean that only flights can be booked with those airlines. If you book the wrong flight with an airline not approved for transit, you will not be able to enter the transit country at all. So, make sure to check whether such regulations exist.

1.5   Vaccinated Travel Lane (VTL-Flights)

More and more airlines offer so-called VTL flights. You may only use these with an accepted vaccination that qualifies you as fully vaccinated. Inform yourself, especially after a mix of vaccinations or for long-distance travels, when someone is considered fully vaccinated at your destination and whether you meet all the requirements to board a VTL flight. You can't get on any VTL flight unvaccinated or if your vaccine is not accepted.

1.6   Vaccination

Within the framework of the entry requirements, please also check the regulations regarding vaccinations. Basically, it can be said: most of you can only travel if you are considered as fully vaccinated against Covid. If not, you will either be completely denied entering a country, or you will have to agree to an extremely overpriced quarantine. Hardly any country grants any easy access to unvaccinated travelers anymore.

However, what fully vaccinated means can be defined differently by each country, and not every country recognizes every vaccine, especially mixed vaccinations with several vaccines. Also, there may be differences between people who have only two or already three or more shots. So, be sure to find out whether your vaccine will be recognized in the desired country and, if necessary, in the country of transit. If you have received a vaccine in Europe, it should be recognized in most countries. With, for example, a Chinese vaccine, however, it can lead to problems, as you might not everywhere qualify as fully vaccinated.

In some cases, countries such as Nepal have banned unvaccinated people, so they are no longer allowed entry to any airport. If you are unvaccinated and staying in a foreign country, be sure to follow the news to see if such a decision is imminent. Otherwise, you might, at some point, no longer be able to leave the country.

2 While Booking Flights

Thanks to Covid, many rules have changed, including those during booking a flight. What's important here is always the country in which you want to travel or the regulations in force there at the time of your entry.

2.1 Money vs. Time

Suppose it is a flight to a country where your ID card or passport is checked or where you generally must present documents (usually but not exclusively international instead of domestic flights). In that case, I strongly advise you to pay for the seat selection, if not already included. I now always book a seat as far to the front exit as possible, as this sometimes saves me *hours* after landing. I was not aware of this in Cambodia and, unfortunately, sat so far in the back that it took me three hours to leave the airport.

Attention: With low-cost airlines, I have recently experienced that an exit was only possible at the back. Even with a very small aircraft, there is often only a staircase at the back. In such a case, it is very frustrating if you have paid for a seat in the front...

2.2   Stay Flexible

It can also be useful to read the sometimes-overwhelming rules for rebooking and cancellation. For example, I had booked a flight with one of the largest airlines, which promised free rebooking, where you might only have to pay the difference for a more expensive day. In the end, I figured out that the logged-in search always showed a plus of 200 USD when requesting a rebooking—if I had logged in and searched for the same flight, it would cost 200 USD less. The promise was nothing more than a nice PR campaign, as any rebooking, no matter which day I chose, would always have cost 200 USD, which then finally made me cancel to get my money back.

2.3   Carry-On Baggage Regulations

In Europe, since Covid, it has very often been the case that only one piece of luggage was allowed onboard. This is especially annoying if you have paid extra for a second piece of luggage. I almost missed my flight to Sweden because I didn't know about this regulation and had to queue at the counter to check-in the second piece of luggage. It is best to research in advance whether such regulations exist for your airline, airport, or country and, if necessary, plan for time before and after.

3   Between Flight Booking and the Flight

In the past, people sat back and relaxed between booking a flight and flying, just looking forward to the upcoming trip. In addition to packing, there was hardly any bureaucratic effort, maybe a visa here or a recommended travel vaccination there, but all in all, the preparation was usually manageable. This is no longer the case, and mistakes can cause a lot of frustration and sometimes very high expenses. That's why you should plan everything very carefully and work with a checklist—you can find it in chapter 9.

Keep in mind that it currently makes no sense to plan early as everything can change quickly. Earlier than ten days before departure, better even, one week, I would not start. Tracking news about your destination always makes sense to see if a major change is pending.

3.1   Current Entry Requirements

Your top priority is to check the current entry requirements. Make sure to do this very shortly before your flight, preferably the day before, including news research or whether changes are planned which come into force on your day of arrival.

Important: You must always check the entry requirements for your destination country, the transport requirements of the airline(s) used, and, if necessary, the transit requirements for your transit country. All three can have different requirements. Remember to always check the *DAT entry requirements*: destination country, airline, transit country.

Example: Which Covid test is necessary?

Your destination country requires a *rapid test*, your airline *does not require* any test, and your transit country requires a *PCR test* for your stopover.

D: Rapid test
A: No test
T: PCR test

You'll need to take a PCR test because of your stopover, plan for the associated costs and deadlines, and find out what kind of PCR test is required—more on that in a moment.

Example: When does the Covid test have to be done?

Your destination country *does not* require a test, your airline requires a test *within 48 hours* of departure, and your transit country requires a test *within 72 hours* before departure.

You must take a test *within 48 hours* before departure and plan for the associated costs.

Very important: The PCR test always beats the rapid test; if one part of DAT requires a PCR test, a rapid test is *no longer* sufficient, even if another DAT part is already fine.

3.2   Happy Testing

If you need to take a Covid test, be sure to pay attention to the time frame. On one of my return flights from outside the EU to Germany, an incredible 90 percent of the passengers in the transit country were separated from our rather large group of onward travelers, as their test was not done within the specified time frame, and this was overlooked during boarding. Everyone had to take an overpriced express PCR test at the airport to be able to take their connecting flights. Please do not blame the hotel or anyone else, as they did. *You* are responsible for your trip, and *you* need to check when your test needs to be taken to meet all regulations.

Very important: Check what time you will receive your result and ask how you get it. You should do both before you are onsite to possibly find another test center. Once I had to pick up the result myself after a few hours. However, in most cases, receiving the documents via e-mail is offered. Make sure that the result is with you before you make your way to the airport. Meanwhile, almost all laboratories offer express tests and results within three hours. These tests are usually very expensive.

Example: Your flight departs on Friday at 1 p.m.

Variant A:

The test must take place within *24 hours* of departure.

You can take the test at 1:01 p.m. on *Thursday* at the earliest. Here, it is not enough to book a test, the result of which reaches you only after 24 hours. For example, you need a test center that will provide you with the result within twelve hours.

Variant B:

The test must take place within *48 hours* of departure.

You can take the test at 1:01 p.m. on *Wednesday* at the earliest. If you go to the test on Wednesday at 5 p.m., you should book a package where the result is there within 24 hours.

Variant C:

The test must take place within *72 hours* before departure.

You can take the test at 1:01 p.m. on *Tuesday* at the earliest. If you go to the test on Tuesday at 5 p.m., you can choose a cheaper option delivering results within 48 hours.

In the meantime, I have done many tests in many countries. Once, my passport number was wrong. Once, the date was wrong (within 48 instead of the allowed 24 hours). I overlooked it because it was correct on one of two documents. I received the corrected version of the test center just in time— if it had closed, I could not have been able to board that flight. A third time, the passport number *and* my date of birth were incorrect. You might think that those centers would get enough money for very few tasks, but apparently, entering the data correctly is a very big challenge. I strongly advise you to check each document three times upon receipt. If necessary, clarify during the test where you can quickly reach someone if there is an error in the test result.

Fortunately, before I left for Thailand, I learned that only an RT-PCR test is accepted for entry. Only then, I learned that PCR is not the same as PCR. In addition to the usual PCR test, there is also the RT-PCR test, the qPCR test, the RT-qPCR test, and the Hot Start PCR test. I'm not going into the distinctions of these tests here, but I just want to let you know that there *are* differences, and you need to figure out which test is needed.

Attention: When leaving for Thailand, the German Federal Foreign Office did *not* have any information on that RT-PCR test but only said PCR. Only my airline provided the correct information. So please check exactly what kind of test is required when planning your trip and don't only trust one source.

In general, it makes sense to compare prices. In Germany, for example, PCR tests are often 130 USD, and a few minutes further away are 50 only USD.

Also, check whether the entry requirements state that a colored signature is necessary. I've read about countries that have a hard time with black-and-white copies. However, I have had no experience with it.

3.3   Covid Insurance

Often, you need health insurance that covers Covid to be allowed to enter. Several health insurance companies offer special Covid insurance, which usually is incredibly expensive. My foreign travel protection in Germany, which costs me very little money annually, also covers Covid up to 100,000 USD for trips of up to eight weeks and is, therefore, valid for all countries I have checked so far. For most countries, coverage amounts between $20,000 and $50,000 are sufficient. I received the corresponding document only on request and covering Covid is not advertised on the website. So, if you already are paying for travel protection abroad, ask if Covid is covered before you overpay elsewhere.

3.4   Digital Covid Forms

Depending on the country, you may need to fill out a digital form to enter. A well-known example is the so-called "Thai Pass" in Thailand, but Austria also had you fill out such a form in the summer of 2021 before entering the country.

Be sure to find out if such a form exists and when it can be filled out. Often, it is only possible shortly before the flight, e.g., three days before. Sometimes, you must upload various documents, such as a passport picture, proof of vaccination, a hotel booking, proof of Covid-covering health insurance, or a Covid test. That's right! As soon as you upload your Covid test, this also limits your possible time window for when you can fill out the form. So, also do some research in advance on what you may have to upload and whether saving the form for later is possible to prevent your session from running out during the filling out process. If a username and password are required, write them down carefully. Check all entries twice before sending them, as incorrect information may lead to the refusal of entry on-site. Also, check whether a printout is necessary.

3.5   Visa Online or "On Arrival"

Since Covid, some countries no longer issue visas "on arrival." This means that even a normal tourist visa may now have to be applied for online in advance, even if this was not the case in the past. In general, there may be changes to the permitted length of stay, which you may be aware of from previous trips. So, be sure to find out if you can get a visa at the airport without applying for it online. Here, too, the rules change often, and it applies as always since Covid: "Expect the unexpected!"

3.6   Quarantine Regulations

Quarantine regulations may apply in your destination country, depending on your vaccination status or its acceptance by the country. Make sure you are aware of these regulations, and, if necessary, book a special quarantine accommodation or a Covid test in advance. The hotel booking website Agoda offers a wide range of quarantine accommodation, which then include, for example, an airport transfer and Covid test—depending on the actual requirements of the country.

Please check these regulations regularly up until your flight, as they are very volatile and can change at any time.

3.7   Covid Apps

Some countries require tracking apps to enter or stay in the country. Especially here, you can hardly rely on the official information, and it makes sense to get in touch with people in the country in advance to find out whether the proof of the app registered to you at check-in is required. Travel forums or social media can be extremely helpful here.

Be aware that you can only travel to those countries with a newer smartphone on which the app needed is running. For example, I could only fly to Malaysia with such an app, and in China, a life without a smartphone is no longer conceivable anyway.

3.8   Printouts

A quick binder is now useful for travel. I use a single transparent slide in which all documents are, but this increases the search effort. Before a flight, it makes sense to sort everything in the order given online, as this often corresponds to the order queried on-site. I've seen documents checked at check-in, at the gate during boarding, at the gate after landing, and at immigration—so make sure you keep them in such a way that you always get to everything quickly.

I would always have the proof of insurance and the proof of vaccination (the last vaccination is sufficient if you are considered fully vaccinated) printed out. Best twice, stored separately.

3.9   Scheduled Departure

You must check with your airline to see if your flight is taking place as planned. I once received a flight cancellation e-mail two weeks before the flight, once an e-mail about changing the departure from morning to a late evening about a week before the flight, and *no* e-mail or any notification when my flight was postponed for a full two days. Just by chance, when I wanted to see if I could postpone the flight myself, I saw this change. Again, traveling requires flexibility these days, so please always check if everything is taking place as planned.

In this context, also pay attention to sufficient financial resources. After an airline canceled my international flight, I was told on request that the refund of almost 200 USD takes up to 180 days. Although the cancellation was not my fault, I had to grant the airline an interest-free loan for almost half a year.

Outrageous but important to consider when planning finan-
cially.

3.10 Flexible Accommodation

According to the overall volatility, I would always make sure to
book accommodation that can be canceled for free, especially
if a flight precedes a booking. In the end, even a false positive
rapid test can prevent your trip if the negative PCR result
comes too late. Booking cancellable accommodation has already saved me an incredible amount of money, as, since
Covid, things simply shift too often, especially flights.

4 72 Hours Before Departure

Congratulations, you have booked and decided on a trip. Before leaving for the airport, especially from about 72 before, you still have a few things to do.

4.1 Entry Requirements and Flight Status

Once, I landed, and the day after, the borders were closed; once, I flew, and the same day, the borders were opened without any tests. If life in a pandemic has shown one thing, it is, above all, how volatile rules are and that everything can change overnight. For example, the Philippines announced its opening for Germans in 2021 but immediately withdrew this announcement. Accordingly, in the three days before departure, you should pay close attention to the current entry requirements and follow the news to see if changes are planned. In total, you have three things that you must check: destination country, airline, and, if necessary, transit country. DAT for short.

It would be a pity to miss something in both directions: you neither want to be sent home due to an entry ban nor pay for a PCR test, where only a rapid test would have been necessary. Almost everyone who landed with me in the Philippines had paid for an expensive PCR test because they missed that recently a rapid test was sufficient. Also, you don't want to pay for a quarantine that is no longer required.

Also, find out again whether your flight is taking place as planned—you can't always rely on receiving information, and I've never seen so many cancellations on the scoreboards at airports in all countries as I have since 2020.

4.2   Covid Test

You may need a Covid test for your trip. Pay attention to the allowed deadlines, which are usually 72, 48, or 24 hours. Your ID or passport number must be correctly listed in the document. If you travel with your passport, this number is required; if you travel with your ID, this number is required. Your name must also not contain any errors and appear as in your used identity document.

Below is the example from before so that you really do not make a mistake in thinking, as I have often experienced.

Example: Your flight departs on Friday at 1 p.m.

I would always add 30 minutes, so I would never go to the test before 1:30 p.m. The following variants nevertheless show the maximum allowed time span.

Variant A:

The test must take place within *24 hours* of departure.

You can take the test at 13:01 on *Thursday* at the earliest.

Variant B:

The test must take place within *48 hours* of departure.

You can take the test at 13:01 on *Wednesday* at the earliest.

Variant C:

The test must take place within *72 hours* before departure.

You can take the test at 13:01 on *Tuesday* at the earliest.

4.3   Final Document Check

In connection with the applicable entry requirements, check your documents one last time, preferably with a self-created checklist. As much as I am against printouts in general, I strongly advise you to have everything printed so that you do not take any risks in terms of technology. Of course, digital backups are highly recommended, preferably offline, so you are never dependent on the internet. At best, you have printed everything twice.

You should have your address in the destination country handy if a special entry document awaits you on the flight. Just in case, take a pen with you.

4.4 Preorder Special Meals

If a meal onboard is included and you generally want to minimize any risks, it makes sense to order a special meal in advance. This usually doesn't cost extra, and you can choose from
a wide range of offers. However, you won't know what your
food will include in advance. Advantage: you receive your food
before everyone else and thus take off your mask when everyone else is still wearing their masks.

4.5 Early Arrival

Before Covid, I always arrived very late at the airport because
I don't like to wait there. Thanks to various negative experiences since Covid, I no longer allow myself such things. With
all the documents that are now checked depending on the
flight, it can take an awfully long time to enter the airport or
get checked in. You don't even have to use a flight where documents are checked—it's enough to stand in a queue where
passengers are affected.

Even if you don't check-in luggage, surprises can await, such as
the need to check in a second piece of hand baggage or the
necessary printout of the boarding pass at the counter. In the
Philippines, I once was told before the security check that digital boarding passes were not valid. So, I had to go to the counter to have them print out my boarding pass and have my hand

luggage weighed. The time that I had not planned because I was traveling without checked baggage.

You don't know what to expect anymore, and if only one person in front of you has incomplete documents, you might already be waiting ten minutes longer. So, *really* make sure to plan enough time at the airport to catch your plane.

5 At the Airport

The airport has also changed a lot in times of a pandemic. However, you can significantly reduce your travel frustration with the following tips.

5.1 Access With Boarding Pass Only

Often, you can only enter an airport with a valid boarding pass—accompanying persons, for example, no longer can come into Asia. Make sure that you always have your ID and boarding pass at hand—you will have to show both several times before your departure, for example, when entering the airport, at check-in, when accessing the security check, on the treadmill of the security check, at passport control, and at the gate.

An example of the extra time required is the airport in Manila in the Philippines, which is only possible with a valid boarding pass and after a baggage scan. Here, endless queues form in front of entrances 1 to 5. Entrance 6, on the other hand, was empty on all three of my flights from there. So, it is almost always worthwhile to go to the last entrance, as almost no one does this. This often saves you half an hour. Basically, you must take this queue into account in your schedule to not miss your plane.

5.2   The Weight of Your Hand Luggage

Since Covid, hand luggage has been weighed more and more often, which must not exceed a certain weight. I still have some filled water bottles in my backpack before the security check, and if the maximum weight is exceeded, I point out that I still have a lot of food and drink in my luggage for the waiting time. Only once was I asked to remove the water, but it still was above the allowed weight. With a friendly smile, I emphasized again that I still had a lot of food in my backpack and was finally allowed to receive my boarding pass.

If something goes wrong here and you are asked to check-in additional baggage for a fee when exceeding the weight limit, you should also plan this time for an emergency if you already know in advance that your luggage weighs more than allowed.

5.3   Unexpected Document Checks and App Installations

Once, I had to fill out a document at the airport before boarding for a domestic flight in the Philippines. This was handed to me at the check-in counter and collected during boarding. It didn't make sense, as I had already flown to the same airport twice in the days before without receiving this document. So take a pen with you. Often, there are documents onboard about your state of health, which must be completed.

On another flight within the Philippines, a so-called "S-Pass" was required, which was requested during boarding. I never researched what exactly this is, but with the help of the staff, like other travelers, I managed to fill out the online form just in time, upload the required proofs, and show the QR code. I found no information about this procedure online in advance, which was only necessary for one flight. Always plan such surprises, and always have all documents at hand or preferably stored digitally so that you can select them directly and upload them in a form or a required app, if necessary.

On a flight to Malaysia, all travelers only learned at the check-in counter that we would not be able to get on board without a tracking app registered with us. They kept our luggage on hold until we were able to present the app showing a green QR code. However, installing the app, registering, and filling out the form for travelers, including document upload, took around 20 minutes for most, as the text message for registration sometimes only came after five minutes. Most of us didn't reach the gate until boarding had just begun. I can only emphasize again and again: be there early enough!

5.4   The Right Gate

Make sure that you regularly check whether the flight is taking place as planned or if the gate has been changed, especially if you arrive early at the airport. Often, the gate is displayed on the screens late but can be viewed much earlier on the airline

or the airport website. Even an employee of the security ser-
vice or the currently not very busy ground staff usually knows
the gate long before the display on the screens at the airport.
Just ask.

6 On the Plane

On the plane, you can relax and don't have so much to do with the chaos and stress of the pandemic—apart from the fact that you may be allowed to sleep with a face mask... Nevertheless, there are a few things to consider.

6.1 Save Time After Landing

If you fly to a country where documents are checked after landing, I strongly advise you to visit a toilet before landing. Your goal should be to get off the plane as soon as possible and be the first to arrive at the document check so you don't have to queue there for hours. Accordingly, you should reduce any distractions at the airport, and this also includes going to the toilet. If necessary, have water given to you again and fill up your water bottle so that you have something to drink during the worst-case long waiting period.

6.2 Prepare the Documents

You must complete at least one document on board depending on the route. My record since Covid was entering Cambodia with a total of three documents. If you have completed documents onboard, add them directly to your remaining documents, which will be checked after landing. I get everything together between landing and disembarkation already in my hand so that I can hurry quickly to the document check and present everything there directly.

6.3   Charging the Phone

If you need your smartphone after arrival, for example, because you only have your documents available digitally to show or an app must be proven for entry, make sure that your battery is sufficiently charged. Especially after international flights with extensive checks, it should last at least a few more hours. A power bank is recommended for flights with low-cost airlines, as it is usually not possible to charge on board.

7 After Landing

Once landed, it is important to be fast in countries with document checks, as I said. Any person you overtake here can save you three to ten minutes that you will spend at the airport. This is followed by information for the time immediately after landing.

7.1 Hurry Up

Do not get distracted and go quickly and directly towards immigration or baggage claim, should you have a document check in front of you. Depending on the country, the procedure can sometimes take ten minutes per person, especially if something is missing.

It takes even longer for "on arrival" tests, where a Covid test is done at the airport, and the result must be waited for. So, if you don't want to queue for hours, your top interest should be to be the first to arrive at the document check counter.

For international travel beyond Schengen, you will be approached for a document check, regular immigration (stamp) if necessary, Covid test, if necessary, or baggage claim, if necessary. Try to minimize this time, and if it does take time, get to know new people during the waiting time. A good starter sentence is always: "Do you remember when traveling still was fun?"

In some cases, there is preferential treatment for people over the age of 70 so that these people do not have to wait for hours. If your companion experiences this treatment, make it clear that you belong together. Normally, you will not be separated.

7.2   Observe Local Regulations

If measures are necessary after landing, such as an "on arrival" test, which is not carried out directly by the authorities, you must take care of them promptly. This can be, for example, a mandatory test in a test center within 24 hours or a privately conducted rapid test after landing on the umpteenth day. Sometimes you must send the results by e-mail to your quarantine hotel and upload them in an app, then the test centers inform the authorities about compliance with the measure and the result. If you must go into quarantine, you will have already organized this in advance, and this usually also includes the transfer to the accommodation from the airport. Be sure to comply with all applicable regulations, as you may have serious difficulties in violating them.

8   Before Leaving Again

The time at your destination is coming to an end, and it's soon time to go back—at least back on a plane. So that it does not get boring, there are again a few things to consider, with which you are already well acquainted. Please also look up the detailed information in chapters 3 and 4 again.

8.1   Entry Requirements

You've been there: DAT is the keyword. For longer stays, inform yourself about changes in between and check the requirements of the destination country, airline, and, if applicable, transit country, i.e., DAT, especially in the last days before departure. On the way back to your home country, an entry registration may be required. Of course, you should also pay attention to possible quarantine regulations again.

8.2   Covid Test

If you need to take a Covid test, ask a hotel or locals if they have a good tip for a cheap and reliable test center. You can also do your own research, but it's always good to know which test center is considered reliable. Please note the applicable deadlines. Once you have your result, check all the data it contains several times, and make sure that your identity document number is included. During the test, get contact details directly in case something is wrong.

It may make sense to opt for a home test variant depending on the country. In the Philippines, the test in my hotel room cost just as much as if I had traveled to the test center for half an hour. Accordingly, I let someone come to me instead of paying twice for a taxi and being on the road forever. In this case, the concierge took over the booking for me, as no one has answered my request via the contact form on the website of the test center to date. Calling is usually the best practice.

8.3   Document Check

The day before your flight, check all the documents you may need and store them properly. Hotels usually print them out to you for free—by the way, even if you don't stay there, they belong to a big chain, and you're a little desperate because time is running out... As I said: asking nice questions helps you very often.

9   Checklist

This checklist will help you to increase your enjoyment of traveling quickly and easily. However, it does not replace reading the individual chapters, as they include more details. Have fun ticking off!

1. **Before booking a flight**

    ☐ Check DAT entry requirements: destination country, airline, transit country, if applicable.

    ☐ Check whether baggage transport is compatible with entry requirements (flights with your own transfer).

    ☐ For price planning, check the cost and necessity of tests in the target country.

    ☐ Check vaccination regulations.

    ☐ Check transit regulations, if necessary.

    ☐ If necessary, check the planned opening of a country.

2. **While booking a flight**

    ☐ Book a seat in the front to save time after landing.

☐ Check the conditions for rebooking and cancellations.

☐ Check hand baggage regulations.

3. Between booking a flight and the departure (start a maximum of ten days before take-off)

☐ Check DAT entry requirements: destination country, airline, transit country, if applicable.

☐ Covid test:

- ○ Check deadlines
- ○ Compare test centers: prices and delivery period of the result
- ○ Check which type of test is necessary
- ○ Check if there are certain requirements for the test result (such as a colored signature)
- ○ Double-check the information contained after receipt of the results, especially the date, ID number, and name

☐ If necessary, take out Covid health insurance.

☐ If necessary, fill out digital Covid entry forms or check deadlines for doing so.

☐ Check visa requirements and, if necessary, apply for an e-visa online.

- ☐ Check quarantine regulations and take precautions if necessary.
- ☐ Check the need for app installations and, if necessary, install and set them up.
- ☐ Print out relevant documents.
- ☐ Book accommodation cancellable to remain flexible in case of changes.
- ☐ Check if the flight is scheduled.

4. 72 hours before departure

- ☐ Check DAT entry requirements: destination country, airline, transit country, if applicable.
- ☐ If necessary, create a document checklist.
- ☐ Check if the flight is scheduled.
- ☐ If necessary, take a Covid test.
- ☐ If necessary, order special meals.
- ☐ Early arrival at the airport.

5. At the airport

- ☐ If necessary, access is only possible with a boarding pass—important if you arrive with an escort.
- ☐ If necessary, weight control of hand luggage.

- [ ] Possible unforeseen document checks or the like.
- [ ] Always check the gate as changes often occur until shortly before boarding.

6. On the plane

- [ ] Before landing, go to the toilet to get through the document check as quickly as possible.
- [ ] Pick up all the documents on the plane.
- [ ] Ensure that your smartphone is fully charged if the evidence is presented digitally.

7. After landing

- [ ] No distractions if a document check is due.
- [ ] Know local regulations, such as mandatory tests upon arrival, and strictly follow them.

8. Before the return or onward journey

- [ ] Check DAT entry requirements: destination country, airline, transit country, if applicable.
- [ ] If necessary, take a Covid test.
- [ ] Compile relevant documents and, if necessary, print them.
- [ ] Look up relevant information from chapters 3 and 4 again.

10 Eleven Basic Tips for Traveling

I don't know if Covid has shaken up some inexperienced people, so they don't wait until their death to travel, but I've never experienced so much awkward travel before. For this reason, I would like to mention a few very basic tips for traveling, which have often saved my day.

10.1 Stay Hydrated

Many travelers had looked at me in amazement in recent months when I unpacked my empty water bottles at the airport instead of buying usually overpriced new ones. At almost all major airports, there are stations where you can get drinking water. In the meantime, refill bottles—who would have thought it—to save plastic. In Asia, hot water is also common. In Europe or countries where you can drink tap water, I usually take a 0.5-liter bottle. A few brands have 0.75-liter bottles, which are more wide than high and therefore fit perfectly under the tap, should there be no water dispenser on-site.

In countries where you can't drink tap water, I usually take two to four bottles with me to always have enough to drink and not have to pay the usually outrageous airport prices. Airport employees always know where the drinking water dispensers are located, so just ask briefly instead of walking and searching for miles. In hot countries, be sure to clean plastic bottles regularly when used multiple times, as bacteria quickly form there.

10.2 Cheap Snacks at the Airport

In Asia and the Middle East, there is usually hot water at the airport. This can be useful for tea if you have a suitable vessel and for noodle cups. As soon as there is hot water at the airport, it can be assumed that at least one grocery store offers noodle cups for extremely little money. Alternatively, you can take one with you if the airport is large enough to safely offer hot water. All international airports in Asia known to me, such as Bangkok, Singapore, Kuala Lumpur, Manila, etc., offer hot water. It always makes sense to take food with you anyway to avoid airport prices.

10.3 Access Money

I have often experienced that credit cards are blocked preventively. To do this, it is often sufficient to use a vending machine where there has already been an attempt at fraud. Traveling through several countries can also prompt a bank to block the card preventively. I know travelers who inform their bank in advance about the planned route. I've never done that myself. Based on my previous experience, I would only ever travel with three credit cards. If I am not traveling alone and know that my companion also takes at least one credit card, I may stay with two. It also makes sense to store these cards separately. I also always backed up the map data in several places in case I needed it. In principle, it makes sense to withdraw a larger sum on arrival in a country due to possible exchange fees and to keep it safe.

If you want to withdraw money at the ATM, you will sometimes be asked whether the withdrawal should be made in the local or home currency. Select only the local currency here! Only then will the daily exchange rate be used. On the other hand, if you choose the home currency, a fixed exchange rate applies, which is always much worse. The same case can occur with card payments. Remember: you are in a certain *country,* so always choose the *national* currency!

10.4 Valuables on the Go

Some countries are less safe than others. Therefore, I often take a tiny wallet or a card case with very little cash and about two expired credit cards. If you are attacked, you can give it out without hesitation, and the perpetrators usually do not want to do anything to you but gain loot. No one checks the expiration date in the event of a robbery, and you get away unscathed. In addition, you save yourself the trouble of having to block your cards.

Where do you store the real cards? Whether in the amusement park in summer without a jacket and bag or when traveling, I almost always have important documents or cash and room cards in my document belly bag under my pants.

10.5 Valuables in the Accommodation

Let's say you're staying in a hotel without a safe and want at least minimal protection for your valuables. Here, it is recommended to lock everything in your suitcase as soon as you leave the room. Usually, the cleaning staff does not have your personal data. Especially in smaller accommodations, however, you never know how well the thing with data protection works. Therefore, I strongly advise against using your date of birth as a code for your suitcase. That would be pretty much the first thing someone would test once they know it to try to open your suitcase. The same applies, of course, to the code of a safe, if available. For example, choose the date of birth of someone close to you with whom you never travel or another number that you do not forget.

10.6 Freezing Cold

On flights, it can get both very hot and very cold. It has also proven to be a good idea to take a vest or sweater with you when traveling to tropical countries and have it handy. Otherwise, you can quickly catch a cold due to the cold air conditioning. I must always decide on a hoodie or bag. I usually opt for the bags because I have a smartphone and headphones at hand. Especially on long flights, I don't want to have anything in my pockets, as this restricts my freedom of movement even more.

Even for visits to cinemas or shopping malls in Asia, the USA, or the Middle East, it can quickly be worthwhile to take warm clothes with you indoors in warm to hot temperatures outside. In spring-like weather in Atlanta in the USA, my ski jacket was necessary in order not to freeze to death in the cinema. Also, at Abu Dhabi airport, I almost froze to death with a five-hour waiting time when I discovered the display of an air conditioner at 16°C or 60°F...

10.7 Stay Connected

For stays outside your home country, a SIM card can quickly be useful to save costs. Ask locals or find out in advance online what the best and cheapest rates are. Don't buy the first SIM card offered at the airport, as these are usually the most expensive. Exceptions confirm the rule, and often you will find fair offers quickly after landing. Be careful not to conclude a contract and have an employee directly conclude the desired tariff. You should know how much GB of data you need, whether the internet is enough, or if you want to make calls.

10.8 Important Things at Hand on the Plane

Do you travel with a suitcase or large backpack in your hand luggage and want to have a few things handy during the flight? You can pack a few smaller items at the gate in a sports bag. You can wear it hidden under a jacket on your back when you board the plane when only one piece of luggage is allowed. Alternatively, you tie it to the backpack or suitcase and place it under the front seat on the plane while you store your large luggage at the top. A belly bag usually also works.

10.9 Quickly Passing the Security Check

Always avoid queues with children and people who are nervous or interested in what's around them because they don't travel often. My first choice is always business travelers and people who clear the laptop out of their luggage at an early stage. They are experienced, don't have to be explained anything, know the rules, and are quick through checking. So that you don't stop everything yourself: almost everywhere in the world, you put out your laptop and the bag of liquids. Nobody is interested in liquids in Asia—I've never had to take them out of my backpack there. Tip on the side: nail scissors are allowed in the hand luggage in Europe but are strictly forbidden in Asia; they end up in the garbage.

10.10 Store Luggage Free of Charge

Are you planning a round trip in a country and would like to do so without a second piece of luggage? Example: you have landed in Bangkok with a large and small backpack and want to explore a few Thai islands before traveling back to Bangkok. In this case, it makes sense to book a room in a hostel or smaller hotel. The operators are usually so nice to store your luggage for weeks free of charge. Alternatively, they charge a smaller amount, and it is nice if you just leave them a little thank you. In Thailand, a girl I met had even stored her two big suitcases in a hostel in Bangkok for two months and didn't have to pay anything for it. Large chains usually charge money and should be avoided for this purpose. This approach works less often in Europe and the US, but asking is always worth it.

10.11 Emergency Information

Take a picture of your ID or passport you're traveling with and keep it stored safely. Note the contact information of the consulate or embassy of your home country in the country you're traveling to. You might also want to store pictures of all other relevant cards you're taking, like health insurance or credit card information.

11 My Travels Since Covid

To end this book, I would like to share with you my travels since Covid, as I am always asked where I have traveled in recent years. As a full-time traveler from Germany, Covid slowed me down for a short time but didn't really stop me. Travel became more complicated from time to time but was mostly possible.

At the beginning of Covid, I was in the process of booking a trip to Egypt. Due to the lockdown talks, I let this be for the time being, and two days later, everything was tight, and the world was extinct. A big cigarette brand advertised stupidly, or funnily, exactly at that time with the sentence, "the world stands still." Of course, I went along with this lockdown, as no one could assess what was happening. At first, I coped surprisingly well with the lockdown because it brought me a longed-for peace, and I could enjoy the exorbitantly good weather in the garden.

After everything slowly reopened in May, I made my first road trip through Germany, where I noticed the differences in the federal states. It wasn't that much fun, which is why I spontaneously decided to spend the summer in Sweden, where I knew others who led a normal life without masks. The summer was fantastic.

In October, I was back in Germany, and soon, the "lockdown light" was approaching, which was supposed to save Christmas but, in the end, lasted until the summer of 2021. At first, I didn't want to travel because few countries had reopened their borders, and the requirements seemed very difficult. I stayed in Germany, although I had almost never been in one place for more than two weeks in years.

In January, I slowly went crazy. I could not and did not want to be in Germany anymore. Neither the warm weather at Christmas nor the sparkling layer of ice that settled over the city in January could significantly improve my mood. It quickly became clear: I must leave, no matter how expensive and complicated. I read through entry requirements, which seemed complex to me at the time, and soon booked a trip to the Maldives, where I never really wanted to go again.

I spent almost two months on a tiny island. I loved how peaceful and quiet it was—the lack of face masks and Covid news. Isolation on that island felt like maximum freedom—and I say that as someone who usually struggles with an island collier on day 1, sometimes even in the UK. Only the previous lockdown made it possible for me to endure it for so long on a small island. On the way back, I spent half a day in Dubai, which was almost extinct in the evening, as I chose a flight with a long stopover to spend a little time here again.

Back in Europe, I soon went on a road trip: Austria, Switzerland, France. Soon after, I flew to Ukraine for a few weeks for a stay in my beloved Kyiv and a huge road trip through the wonderful country. Shortly afterward, I moved into a penthouse in Spain for a few months, from where I was able to admire the sunrise over the sea every morning and the mostly bright pink sunset every evening. I ended my stay with a road trip through Portugal and France and a visit to my beloved Disneyland Paris. Immediately afterward, I finally went back to London for a longer time—I really missed this city and the people very much.

In December 2021, I finally set off for Asia because I just don't like Europe for more than a few days in winter. I spent two months in Thailand, one in Cambodia, and one in the Philippines. My travel experiences finally made me want to write this book during my stay in Malaysia.

Between March 2020 and April 2022, I have traveled the following 16 countries:

- Germany
- Luxembourg
- Sweden
- Maldives
- UAE
- Austria
- Switzerland
- France
- Ukraine
- Spain
- Portugal

- UK
- Thailand
- Cambodia
- Philippines
- Malaysia

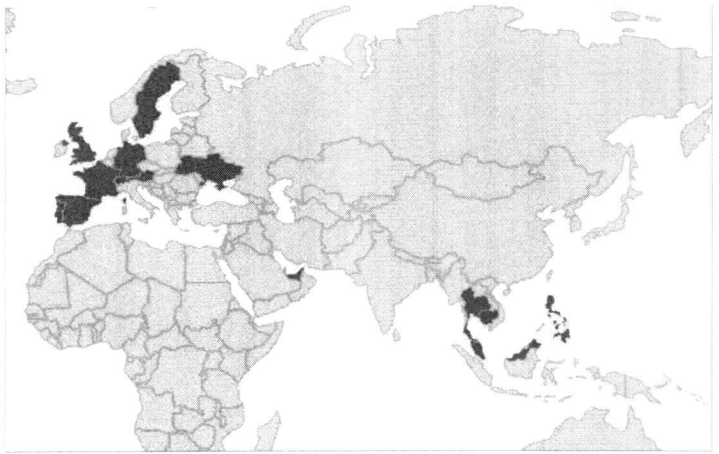

Printed in Poland
by Amazon Fulfillment
Poland Sp. z o.o., Wrocław

90746364R00034